Scary Creatures
LIZARDS

Written by
Gerard Cheshire

Created and designed
by David Salariya

BOOK HOUSE

Author:

Gerard Cheshire has written many books
on natural history, and over the past twelve years has
cultivated an excellent reputation as an author and
editor. He now lives in Bath, England, with his wife
and three sons.

Artists:
John Francis
Robert Morton
Carolyn Scrace
Nicholas Hewetson
Catherine Constable

Series Creator:

David Salariya was born in Dundee,
Scotland. In 1989 he established The Salariya Book
Company. He has illustrated a wide range of books
and has created many new series for publishers in the
UK and overseas. He lives in Brighton with his wife,
illustrator Shirley Willis, and their son.

Editor: Stephen Haynes

Editorial Assistants:
Rob Walker, Tanya Kant

Picture Research:
Mark Bergin, Carolyn Franklin

Photo Credits:

t=top, b=bottom

Cadmium: 5, 11, 13, 29t
Corel Professional Photos: 20, 21t
Corbis: 19
John Foxx Images: 6, 10, 12, 29b
Daniel Heuclin/NHPA: 9
Ernie Janes/NHPA: 15
Mountain High Maps/© 1993 Digital
   Wisdom Inc.: 22–23
PhotoDisc: 21b

Published in Great Britain in 2008 by
Book House, an imprint of
The Salariya Book Company Ltd
25 Marlborough Place, Brighton BN1 1UB

S A L A R I Y A

A catalogue record for this book is available
from the British Library.

HB ISBN: 978-1-906370-15-2
PB ISBN: 978-1-906370-09-1

Printed in China

Visit our website at **www.book-house.co.uk**
for **free** electronic versions of:
You Wouldn't Want to be an Egyptian Mummy!
You Wouldn't Want to be a Roman Gladiator!
Avoid Joining Shackleton's Polar Expedition!
Avoid Sailing on a 19th-Century Whaling Ship!

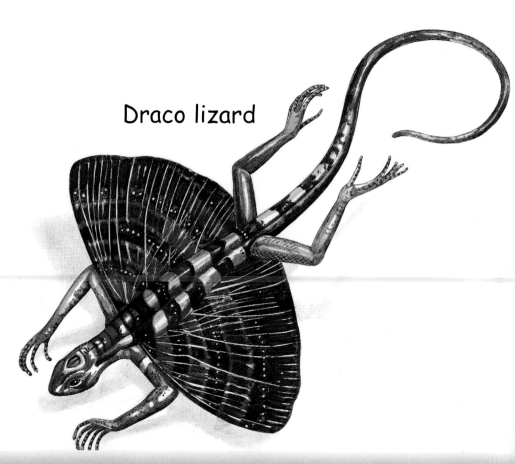

Draco lizard

PAPER FROM
SUSTAINABLE
FORESTS

Contents

Thorny devil

What are lizards?

Lizards belong to a class of **cold-blooded** animals called **reptiles**, along with snakes, tortoises, crocodiles, alligators and turtles. They have scaly skin which provides protection from enemies and stops them losing water from their bodies. As lizards grow, they shed or **moult** their old skins because the scales cannot stretch. Baby lizards hatch from soft-shelled eggs.

Are these animals lizards?

Snakes have no legs and no eyelids. They can separate their jawbones to swallow very large **prey**.

Gaboon viper

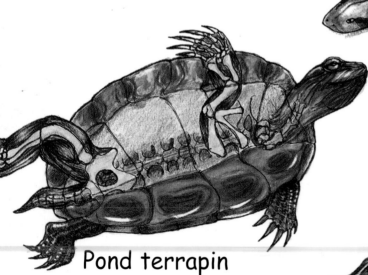

Caimans, alligators and crocodiles are the same shape as lizards but they are designed for life in water, with webbed toes and sharp teeth for catching their prey.

Pond terrapin

Caiman

Tortoises, turtles and terrapins have hard shells called carapaces. These are made of bone with scales over the top.

No, none of these animals are lizards.

Did You Know?

Newts and salamanders are often mistaken for lizards, because they have the same shape. But they are not reptiles, and have no scales. They are **amphibians**, just like frogs and toads.

The scales of this Galápagos land iguana can be seen clearly.

Do all lizards lay eggs?

All baby lizards develop inside eggs, but not all lizards actually lay their eggs. Some lizards keep the eggs inside their bodies until they hatch, so it looks as though they are giving birth to live babies, as mammals do.

X-Ray Vision
Hold the next page up to the light and see what's inside the eggs.
See what's inside

Iguanas mating

Do lizards have legs?

Most lizards have four legs, but a few **species** have just two legs or no legs at all. This is because they burrow under the ground like worms. Legs would only get in the way, so they have evolved to lose them. This makes them look very like snakes.

Lizards without legs include slow-worms and glass-snakes. They have hard noses so that they can burrow with their heads, and they move by making waves or ripples along their bellies.

Mole lizards and some worm lizards have just two front legs for digging. Skinks have four legs, but they are often so small that they serve no useful purpose.

Worm lizard

What's so special about a lizard's tail?

Many small lizards are able to lose their tails on purpose when attacked by **predators**. This is called **autotomy**, which means 'self-cutting'. The puzzled predator is left with a wriggling tail while the lizard makes its getaway. The lizard is not harmed, and can grow a new tail.

Green iguana

You might think that lizards would be better off without tails in the first place, but they use them for balance and for swimming. Some lizards have very short tails; they have a lifestyle which means they don't need to balance or swim.

Chameleon

Did You Know?

Lizards can move their eyes independently, swivelling each one in a different direction. This is easy to see in chameleons, because they have such bulging eyes.

Why do lizards lie in the sun?

Unlike humans and other mammals, lizards are cold-blooded. This means that their body has the same temperature as the air around it. They find it difficult to move about until they have warmed themselves up. They **bask** in sunshine until their bodies reach a temperature where they are ready for action. In places where the sun isn't always hot, lizards tend to be darker in colour, so that their scales can absorb as much energy from the sun as possible. In very hot places, they often have to cool off in the shade.

In places where it gets too cold for lizards to remain active, they have to hibernate for the winter.

Did You Know?

The European common lizard can survive even in the Arctic Circle, where the ground remains frozen all the year round. It hibernates in the winter, allowing its body temperature to fall below zero degrees Celsius.

Where do lizards prefer to live?

Lizards thrive in tropical regions because the warm climate suits them. They don't need to spend so much time sunbathing, because they are already warm enough to go about their daily business. In fact, it is often warm enough for them to be active even at night, with no sunlight at all.

Lizards prefer to live in warm places.

Lacerta lizards often bask on rocks to warm themselves up.

What are the oldest lizards?

Tuataras are not actually lizards, but they are the oldest lizard-like animals alive today. They are described as 'living fossils', because all the other animals of this type died out millions of years ago. They have an organ called a **third eye** on top of their head, and they have no ear holes – but they can hear.

Did You Know?

Animals related to the tuatara lived around 200 million years ago, when dinosaurs were still alive. Now tuataras are an **endangered species**, found only in New Zealand. They can live to be over 100 years old.

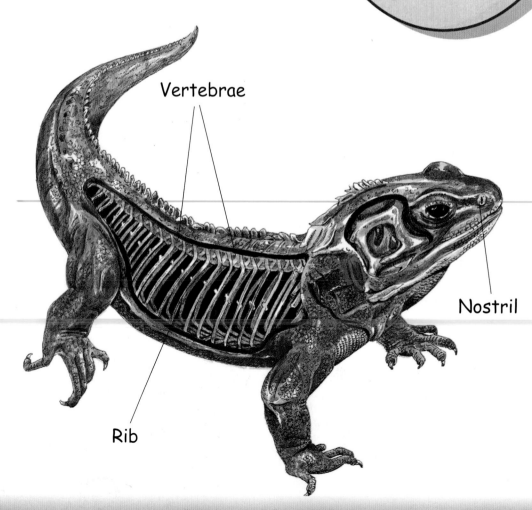

Vertebrae

Nostril

Tuatara

Rib

Slow-worms are probably the longest-lived of the small lizards. They live in burrows underground where they are unlikely to be injured or eaten by enemies. They can live for more than 30 years, which is a long time for a lizard.

But Komodo dragons (see pages 18–19) can live for 50 years or more. They are the largest lizards in the world and they have no natural enemies. Large animals tend to grow more slowly and live longer anyway – provided they don't get ill, injured or eaten.

Komodo dragon

Slow-worm

Are lizards related to dinosaurs?

The word *dinosaur* means 'terrible lizard'. But dinosaurs were not really lizards. In fact, scientists now think that their nearest living relatives are birds. Dinosaurs had bird-like skeletons, and they may have been warm-blooded, too. Today's lizards are probably descended from an early type of lizard that lived at the same time as the dinosaurs.

Pteranodon

Diplodocus

Deinonychus

Modern pigeon

Stegosaurus

Modern crocodile

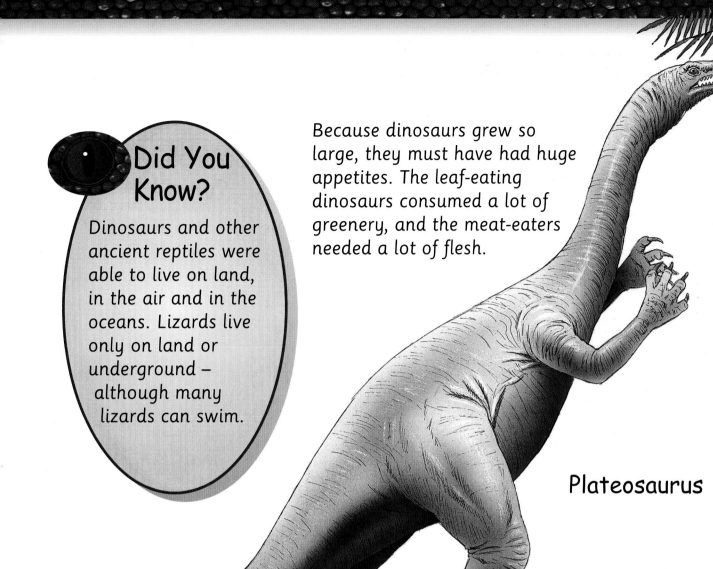

Did You Know?

Dinosaurs and other ancient reptiles were able to live on land, in the air and in the oceans. Lizards live only on land or underground – although many lizards can swim.

Because dinosaurs grew so large, they must have had huge appetites. The leaf-eating dinosaurs consumed a lot of greenery, and the meat-eaters needed a lot of flesh.

Plateosaurus

What happened to the dinosaurs?

Some scientists think that as the world's climate changed over time, some of the plants dinosaurs ate could no longer grow. The dinosaurs slowly began to die off. Then a giant meteorite hit the Earth. The dust from this collision may have blocked out the sun, causing other plants to die off. Without any plants for food, dinosaurs eventually died out.

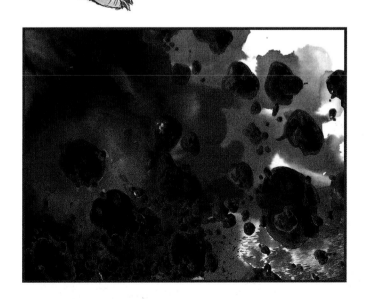

Meteorite impact

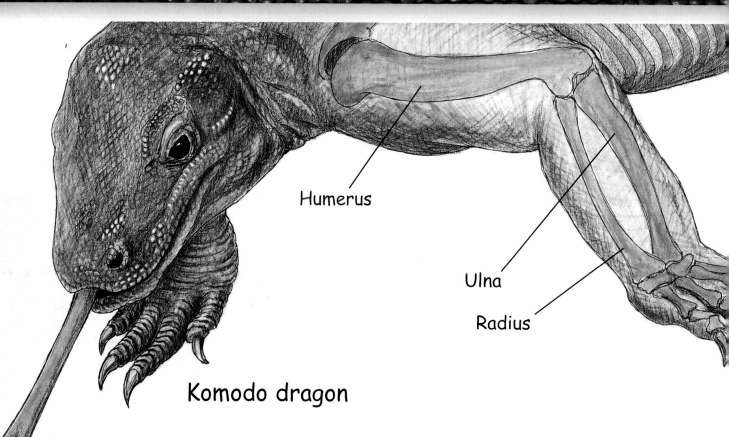

Humerus

Ulna

Radius

Komodo dragon

Are there really dragons?

When European explorers began to discover distant lands, they came home with fantastic tales of giant creatures. Perhaps they had seen real animals such as the giant squid or the elephant bird of Madagascar, which is now extinct.

No-one has ever seen a flying, fire-breathing dragon – but there is a real animal called a Komodo dragon. It is a very large type of monitor lizard that lives on a number of islands in South-East Asia.

A fairytale dragon

Komodo dragon

These scary lizards can grow up to 3 metres (10 feet) in length. They are formidable predators and have been known to attack and eat humans. Their saliva contains nasty bacteria that infect the animals they bite. This means that escaping prey animals can be followed until they become too sick to run any further. The unfortunate victims are then torn to pieces and swallowed up.

Female Komodo dragons have the ability to lay fertile eggs without mating. This means that a single female could swim across to another island and start a new colony there all by herself.

What do lizards eat?

Some lizards are herbivores: they eat plant matter, such as leaves, fruit and flowers. Others are insectivores: they eat insects and other **invertebrates**, such as spiders, worms and slugs. Many are **carnivores**: they eat larger animals such as frogs, birds and small mammals. A few species are omnivores, eating a mixture of plant and animal matter.

Collared lizard eating an insect

Gila monster

Did You Know?

Lizards don't usually need to drink, as they get enough moisture from their food.
The thorny devil (or moloch), a lizard that lives in Australian deserts, can drink dew by allowing it to flow over its body into its mouth.

Iguanas are mostly herbivorous. They eat all kinds of soft plant matter, but baby iguanas often eat invertebrates too, as they are too small to reach leaves and fruit. Geckos are insectivores, snapping up bugs whenever they come close enough. Monitors are carnivorous lizards. They often hunt for mammals and birds by digging in the ground or climbing trees. Chameleons are omnivores. They shoot out their long, sticky tongues to catch insects, but they also bite off leaves and buds.

Jackson's chameleon

Where do lizards live?

Lizards are found around the world. The only places they don't live are where it is too cold, such as on mountain tops and at the North and South Poles. Also, there are no lizards in the oceans.

Iguana

Gila monster

Around the middle of the Earth is the **equatorial** or tropical region, which is always hot. On either side of this band are **temperate** regions, where temperatures gradually get cooler. Lizards are found in all of these areas.

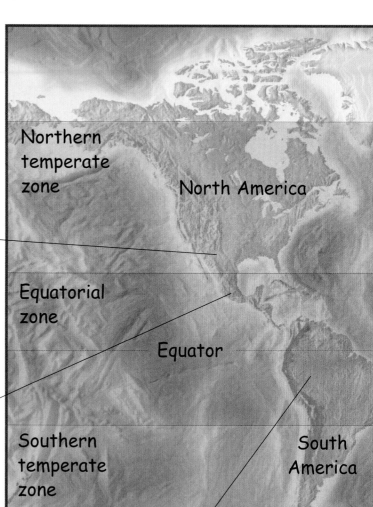

Northern temperate zone

North America

Equatorial zone

Equator

Southern temperate zone

South America

Antarctica

Tegu

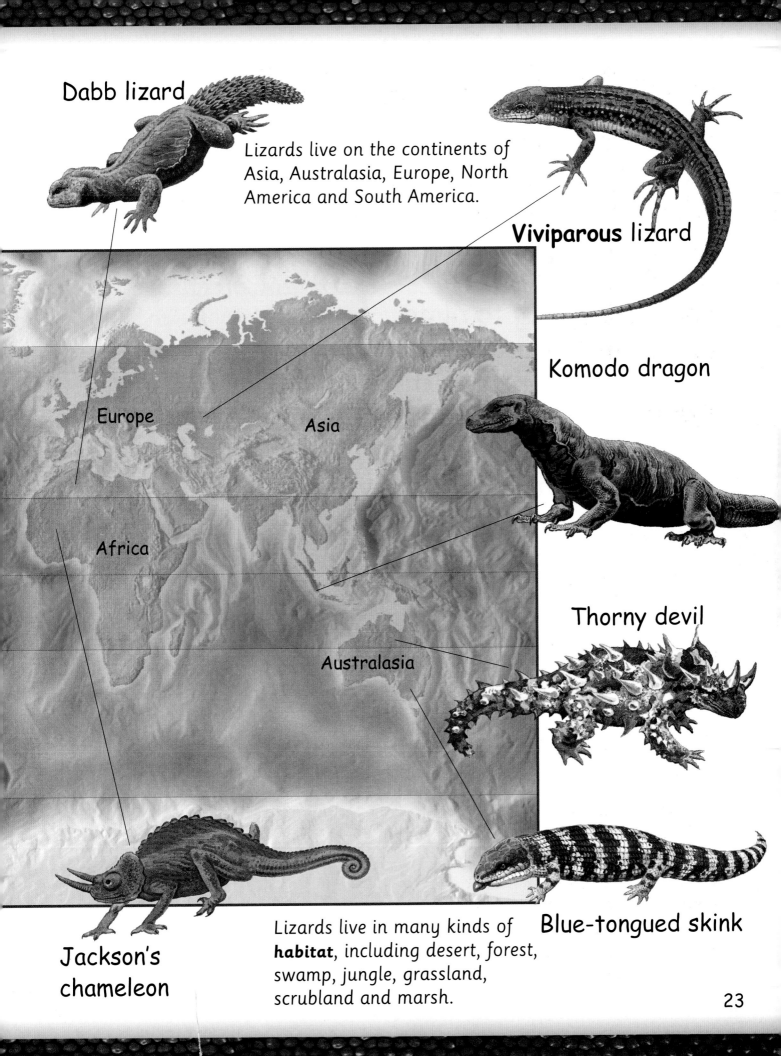

Dabb lizard

Lizards live on the continents of Asia, Australasia, Europe, North America and South America.

Viviparous lizard

Europe

Asia

Africa

Australasia

Komodo dragon

Thorny devil

Jackson's chameleon

Lizards live in many kinds of **habitat**, including desert, forest, swamp, jungle, grassland, scrubland and marsh.

Blue-tongued skink

Can lizards fly?

No, lizards cannot really fly. They can't take to the air and remain airborne. But there are some kinds that are known as 'flying lizards', because they have the ability to glide. These are the draco lizards from South-East Asia. The word *draco* actually means 'dragon'. They are called this because mythical dragons are supposed to be able to fly.

X-Ray Vision

Hold the next page up to the light and see how the lizard glides.

See what's inside

The wings of bats and birds are actually their front legs, which have evolved into a shape suitable for flying. Draco lizards are quite different: their wings are made from the animal's ribs. They stretch out like a fan on each side of the body and are covered with skin. Draco lizards use their wings to glide from one tree to another in search of food, without needing to walk on the ground.

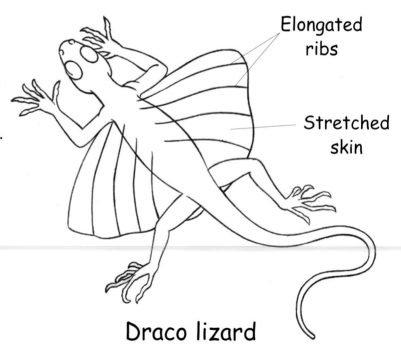

Elongated ribs

Stretched skin

Draco lizard

This drawing of a draco lizard
is a little larger than life size.

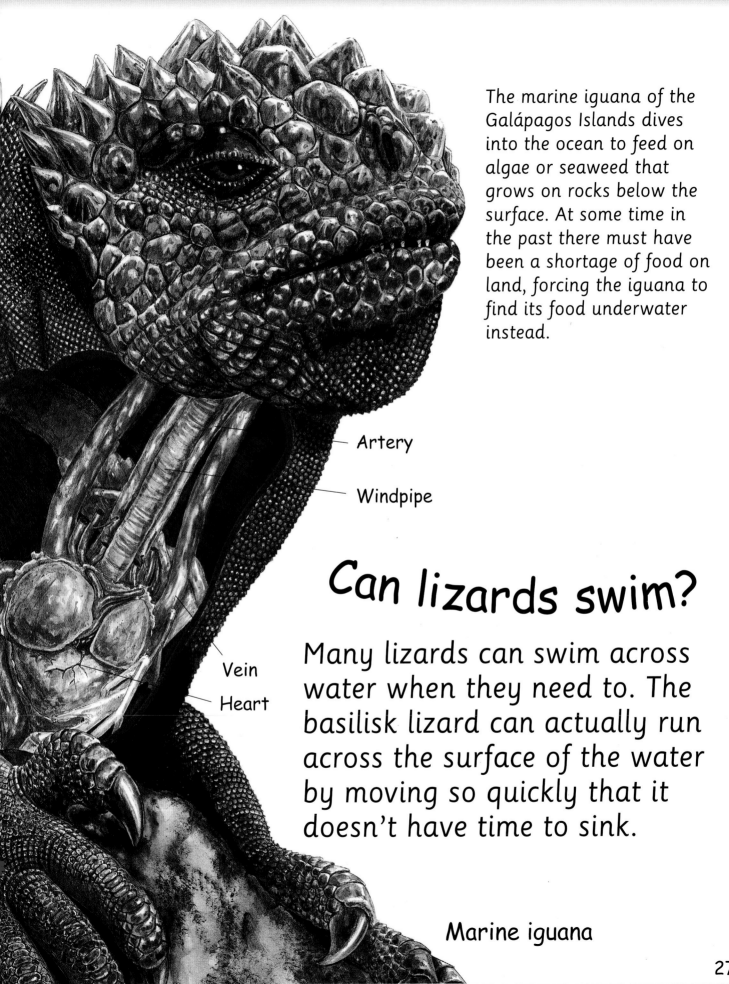

The marine iguana of the Galápagos Islands dives into the ocean to feed on algae or seaweed that grows on rocks below the surface. At some time in the past there must have been a shortage of food on land, forcing the iguana to find its food underwater instead.

Artery

Windpipe

Vein

Heart

Can lizards swim?

Many lizards can swim across water when they need to. The basilisk lizard can actually run across the surface of the water by moving so quickly that it doesn't have time to sink.

Marine iguana

Can lizards walk upside down?

Very small creatures such as flies can walk upside down because they have tiny hooks on their feet that latch onto smooth-looking surfaces. Some lizards, called geckos, can walk upside down, too. Instead of hooks, their toes are covered in thousands of microscopic hairs. These are so fine that they make a special bond with the surface, rather like a magnet attracted to iron. Geckos have to peel each foot off again in order to move around. They are so good at climbing that they can even walk up windows.

Gecko

The tiny hairs on the gecko's toes are arranged into ridges, almost like human fingerprints.

In the wild, geckos use their special feet to walk on slippery leaves and on the ceilings of caves, where they hunt for insects and spiders.

Other lizards climb by using the hooked claws on their toes. They can climb up or down by twisting their feet round so that their claws hold them in position. This method of climbing is fine for rough surfaces such as rocks and tree trunks, but it wouldn't work on smooth surfaces.

Green iguana

Did You Know?

Lizards shed or moult their skin in bits and pieces. As the new skin grows underneath, the old skin splits and peels away, making the lizard look rather scruffy for a few days until it has all fallen away.

Lizard moulting

Lizard facts

The Komodo dragon is the largest lizard, at 3 metres (10 feet) long.

Some geckos in Madagascar have ragged edges to their bodies and legs, which makes them difficult to spot when lying on tree trunks. They also have tails the same shape as their heads, so that predators are not sure which end to bite.

Horned lizards from the USA can squirt blood from their eyes to put predators off eating them. They also have sharp, horn-like scales that make it difficult for predators to bite them.

The gila monster, found in the USA, is one of the few lizards that have a venomous (poisonous) bite. It is a desert lizard, so it is important that it kills its prey, otherwise it might die of starvation. Another venomous species is the Mexican beaded lizard. Some Australian lizards have mildly poisonous bites.

The frilled lizard of Australia has a neck ruff or frill which it can extend to make itself look bigger and scarier than it really is. The orange and blue ruff startles predators while the lizard sprints away on its hind legs.

The earless monitor is one of the very few lizards adapted to hunting in fresh water. It lives in the swamps of Sarawak in Malaysia, where it feeds on invertebrates, fish and amphibians. Other lizards that spend part of their time in the water are the sailfin lizards and the water dragons of the Australasian region.

Most lizards use their body colour for camouflage, but chameleons can actually change their colour. They can use this to express their feelings to one another.

The smallest lizard is the dwarf gecko. It is only 16mm (⅝ inch) long and lives on a small Caribbean island.

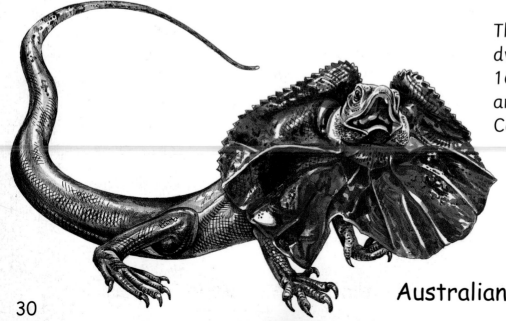

Australian frilled lizard

Glossary

amphibian An animal that lives mostly on land but breeds in water.

autotomy The ability which lizards have to lose their tail and grew a new one.

bask To lie in the sun in order to get warm.

carnivore Any animal that eats the flesh of other animals as its main food source.

cold-blooded Having a body temperature that goes up and down to match the surrounding temperature.

endangered species An animal which is in danger of dying out because there are so few individuals left alive.

equatorial Belonging to the equator – the part of the Earth that is furthest from the Poles and has the hottest temperatures.

habitat The place where an animal naturally lives.

hibernate To go into a very deep sleep during the winter.

invertebrate An animal with no backbone.

moult (or **slough**) To shed an old skin; most reptiles do this from time to time as they grow.

predator Any animal that kills and eats other animals.

prey Any animal that is hunted by other animals for food.

reptile A cold-blooded vertebrate animal with scaly skin, such as a lizard, a snake, a crocodile or a tortoise.

species A group of animals that look alike, behave in the same way, and can breed together.

temperate Neither very hot nor very cold.

third eye An eye-like organ in the head of some reptiles. It is not a real eye, and scientists are not entirely sure what it is for.

vertebrate Any animal with a backbone.

viviparous Giving birth to live babies, rather than laying eggs.

Sticky tongue

Yemenese chameleon

Index